No Cowards Here

Compiled by Gordon Parke

Illustrated by
Anthony Stileman

SCRIPTURE UNION,
47 Marylebone Lane,
London W1M 6AX

Also by Gordon Parke:
Coffins for Traitors

© Scripture Union 1974
First published 1974

ISBN 0 85421 450 X

Photoset in Malta,
by St Paul's Press Ltd

Printed in Great Britain by
A. McLay & Co. Ltd. Cardiff and London

Contents

Foreword

This book has been written by four teachers from Sussex. Hugh Lowries has written the stories about Patrick, Peter, and Margaret Hayes; Robert Shimwell has written the stories about Esther, Daniel and 'Operation Auca': John Waters wrote about David and Goliath, Paul, and Gladys Aylward: while I wrote the others. We chose these stories because they were all about people we admire. We hope you will like them and will want to read more about them.

Gordon Parke

The Young Giant Slayer

Israel was at war, but there was very little actual fighting taking place. Their enemies, the Philistines, were on the mountains on one side of a small valley, while King Saul and the Israelites were on the other side. At this time the Philistines were a very powerful nation and their soldiers were well trained, well supplied, and well armed. By contrast, the Israelite army was quite untrained and had almost no supplies. Even so, it looked as though the Philistines did not want to get involved in a real battle. For the moment, as long as the Israelites did not attack, the Philistines were happy.

The valley separating the two armies had steep sides, and there was a little stream running through the middle. It would have been foolish for the Israelites to attack the Philistines, and if the Philistines wanted to attack the Israelite army they would have to cross the valley and scramble up the other side. As the soldiers would be wearing their heavy armour, they would be slow and soon get tired. It would be madness if the Philistines attacked. There was absolute stalemate. No fighting, no killing, nothing at all.

The Philistines had a champion named Goliath. He was a giant of a man, over nine feet tall. He wore a bronze helmet on his head and his armour was also made of bronze. He carried a huge spear.

Goliath came out from the Philistine soldiers, with his shield-bearer in front of him, and stood in full view of the Israelite army. Goliath shouted, 'Choose one of your soldiers and let him come down to me. If he is able to fight with me and kill me, then the Philistines will be your servants, but if I kill him then you will be our servants and serve us.' When King Saul and the Israelite soldiers heard what Goliath said they were very frightened. Nobody wanted to go and fight the Philistine giant. Every morning and every evening for forty days Goliath shouted out his challenge to the Israelites, and every day the Israelites became more and more uneasy and wondered what the Philistines would do if nobody accepted Goliath's challenge.

Jesse was a very old man who lived up in the mountains near Bethlehem. His three eldest sons, Eliab, Abinadab, and Shammah, were in the Israelite army, but his youngest son, David, was still living at home. It was David's job to look after the family flock of sheep. He quite enjoyed doing this, but sometimes he thought about his brothers in the army and wished that he could be with them. He didn't want to be a shepherd, he wanted to be a soldier. Not that David's job was easy. Far from it. Quite often he had to chase away the wild animals which attacked the flock, and he had even killed lions and bears. Even so, David was rather envious of his brothers.

One day Jesse asked David to take some food to his brothers. There were a bag of grain and ten loaves of bread, as well as ten beautiful cheeses for the commanding officer.

Next morning David got up very early. He arranged for someone to look after the sheep, and then set off down the mountain on the start of his journey. David was in a hurry. This was his chance to see all the soldiers and he was going to make the most of it.

He reached the Israelite camp just as the army was going out to take up its position and was raising the war cry. He was in time. Now he might even see some fighting. The Israelites and the Philistines drew up their ranks opposite each other. David left his things with the quartermaster and ran up to the soldiers to look for his three brothers. He soon found them. There were so many questions he wanted to ask. How were they? Had they done much fighting? Why wasn't anyone fighting at the moment?

While David was talking to his brothers, the Philistine champion, Goliath, moved out from the enemy ranks and shouted out his challenge. Although by now the Israelites were used to this, some of the soldiers near David were so frightened that they ran back to the safety of the camp. David stood and stared at this giant. He certainly was tall, but why was everybody so frightened of him? After all, he was only a man, just like everybody else. As David looked at Goliath something stirred inside him. Did God want him to go and fight Goliath? No! David was only a boy! He wouldn't have a chance against a trained soldier. But if none of the Israelite army would accept

Goliath's challenge, then who would? The more David thought about it, the more he wanted to accept Goliath's challenge. Goliath might beat him, but David put his trust in God. Now he was sure that God wanted him to fight. Some of the nearby soldiers were looking at him. 'I'll kill Goliath,' said David. The soldiers laughed, but then they stopped. There was something about this boy which made them take him seriously.

The soldiers told David that King Saul had promised to reward the person who killed Goliath. Saul had said that he would give the person a lot of money, and even allow him to marry his daughter.

His brothers overheard what David was saying to the soldiers and were very angry. 'Go back to the sheep,' shouted Eliab. 'I know why you've come here. You just want to see some fighting. Stop this silly talk and go back home. This is no place for a boy like you.' What could David do? After all, Eliab was his eldest brother. He turned away, but carried on talking to the other soldiers.

Soon the whole camp was talking about the shepherd boy who said he would kill Goliath. When King Saul heard the news, he sent for David. David came at once. 'Sir, I'm not scared of Goliath. Let me go and kill him.' Saul smiled. 'Good for you, my boy, but you can't go out and fight this man. You're only a child and Goliath has been a fighting man all his life. You wouldn't have a chance.'

David was not too discouraged at this, and he

told Saul about how he had killed the lions and bears that had attacked his flock of sheep. 'If I can kill lions and bears, then I'm sure I can kill Goliath. If God helped me before, he'll help me now.'

Saul was impressed, and eventually he agreed to let David face Goliath. He even let David borrow his armour and sword, but David was so uncomfortable in the armour that he had to take it off, and he didn't take Saul's sword because it was too heavy. Instead he picked up his staff and walked forward. He was on his way to try and kill Goliath, and all the Israelite army was watching him. Goliath was a trained soldier, and he was much bigger and stronger than David, but David wasn't too frightened. After all, he was doing what God wanted him to do and that was the important thing. He was fighting for what was right, and he had God on his side.

David started off down the side of the valley. Goliath was still on the other side shouting out his challenge. All at once Goliath saw David coming towards him. At first he could hardly believe his eyes. Were the Israelites expecting him to fight a boy? He didn't want to kill a boy, he wanted to kill one of Israel's most famous soldiers. Goliath was angry.

David reached the stream. He bent down and picked up five smooth stones and put them in his little shepherd's bag. Slowly he stood up and stared at the giant. His legs began to shake and he wished that he hadn't been quite so keen to go and kill Goliath. He felt the stones in his bag, and then took out his shepherd's sling. 'God, be with me,' said David. 'You helped me kill the lion and the bear. Please help me to kill this giant.'

Goliath, with his shield-bearer in front of him, walked towards David. He looked David up and down and shouted out, 'Am I a dog that you come against me with sticks?' By now Goliath was really annoyed. He swore at David, and said, 'Come on, then, if you fight me I will give your flesh to the birds of the air and the beasts of the field.' David shouted back, 'You come to me with a sword and a spear, but I come to you in the name of the Lord of Hosts, the God of the army of Israel. The Lord will deliver you into my hand, and I shall kill you and cut your head off, and leave your body to the wild animals. Then everyone will know that there is a God in Israel, and that swords and spears don't bother him!'

At this Goliath stepped forward, and walked towards David. David looked at the Philistine, and ran forward to meet him. Quickly he put his hand into his shepherd's bag, took out one of his stones, and slipped it into his sling. Carefully he took aim. Goliath, in all his shining armour, stood watching. Once more David muttered a quick prayer. 'God, please help me.' David swung his arm and watched the stone as it flew through the air. It looked a good shot. David watched as it struck Goliath on the forehead. He watched as Goliath crashed to the ground and lay still. In a flash David ran to where the Philistine lay and stood over the motionless figure. Bending down, he hauled Goliath's sword out of its scabbard, killed him, and then hacked the giant's head from off his great shoulders. David had killed Goliath, and the Philistines were defeated.

As soon as the Philistine soldiers saw that their champion was dead, they turned and ran. The cheering Israelites chased after them, and they also raided the deserted Philistine camp.

Once again David's courage and his belief in God had saved the day. This time David had saved the Israelites from the Philistines, just as he'd saved his sheep from the attacks of wild animals.

David had this courage all his life, and later he used it to protect and care for his people when he was king.

One Against Four Hundred

Ahab was a selfish and weak king and his reign was not a happy time for the people of Israel. He found it hard to choose the right way rather than the easy way. And in his reign there were few who held to the right way.

The few, however, included two remarkable characters – Elijah and Micaiah.

Ahab was not helped by his wife, Jezebel, a determined and bloodthirsty woman. We can see what she was like from the way in which she acquired for Ahab a vineyard he wanted very much.

Naboth owned this vineyard, and when Ahab tried to buy it from him, he refused. He did not want to part with a plot of land that had been in his family for generations. Ahab then acted just like a spoilt child. He went and lay on his bed and sulked and would not even eat.

Jezebel got the story out of him. She did not sulk. She took action and at once wrote to the nobles and important people in Jezreel to arrange a trial. The queen's orders were quite clear and so was the result of the trial. The only man who did not know of all the queen's arrangements was the innocent Naboth.

Two witnesses were produced. They were willing to say anything as long as they were paid enough. They told the judges that they had heard Naboth saying evil things about God and Ahab. That was enough. Naboth was dragged out of Jezreel and stoned. The nobles (not a very good name for them) proudly sent a messenger to Jezebel to say that Naboth was safely dead. Ahab got his vineyard, and it was made clear to everyone that it was not a good idea to defy the king or the queen. There were, however, two who were brave enough – a famous prophet, Elijah, who challenged Ahab about it, and Micaiah.

Ahab soon wanted something else, rather bigger than Naboth's vineyard. This was the border town of Ramoth-Gilead, which was in the territory of Syria, Israel's old enemies. It was a tough task and he decided to ask Jehoshaphat, king of his countrymen in Judah, to join him in the attack. Now Jehoshaphat had a faith in God, and wanted to find out if Ahab's plan was right. Ahab never seemed quite sure whether he believed in God or not, but he was happy enough to deal with Jehoshaphat's worries. He had a vast number of prophets who were experts at deciding what God wanted, and even more expert at deciding what Ahab (and perhaps even Jezebel) wanted. At any rate Ahab was confident that he would receive the go-ahead he so much wished for.

He was right. Without hesitation, four hundred of Ahab's prophets recommended him to attack Syria. They promised that the Lord would deliver it into his hand.

Even this, however, did not re-assure Jehoshaphat, who said, 'Isn't there any other prophet of the Lord that we can ask?' Ahab must have felt Jehoshaphat was hard to please. If 400 prophets wouldn't satisfy him, what would? Anyway, it was a question he didn't want to answer. There were a few troublesome prophets in Israel like Elijah and Micaiah who rarely told him what he wanted to hear, and often had the nerve to tell him he was doing wrong. But he could see Jehoshaphat was not satisfied, and reluctantly he told him of Micaiah. 'I'll send a messenger to him to get his views,' he promised Jehoshaphat. He made sure he had a few words with his messenger before he set out.

The two kings, magnificently dressed in their finest robes, were sitting in the square inside the main gates of the town of Samaria. The townspeople were gathered around. Zedekiah, leader of the four hundred prophets, saw his chance of making a big impression on Ahab, the inhabitants and this doubting king of Judah, Jehoshaphat. Solemnly he advanced into the square with all eyes upon him. In his hands something glinted in the sun. He bowed before the kings, and then with a flourish he held up in front of him two gleaming horns of iron. Then in a loud voice he proclaimed, 'This is what the Lord says. With these horns you will push the Syrians backwards till you have destroyed them.' And then in a great male voice chorus of four hundred prophets came the chant, 'Go to Ramoth-Gilead and win, for the Lord will give you victory.' Everyone watching must have been impressed, even Jehoshaphat.

In the meantime, Ahab's messenger arrived at the house of Micaiah. He had a tricky task and probably knew it. He explained the situation to Micaiah and then added, 'Look here, Micaiah, before you rush in with your answer, let me give you a friendly word of advice. We don't want any trouble and you know what king Ahab is like when he is crossed. All the king's prophets are in agreement over this, so don't be the odd man out. Tell the king that the Lord wants him to attack the Syrians, there's a good fellow.'

Micaiah answered, 'I will tell the king the words that God speaks to me.' The messenger had to be satisfied with this and he led Micaiah to Samaria, where the kings were still sitting in state. Ahab recognised Micaiah without, we may guess, much enthusiasm.

'Ah, Micaiah,' he said, 'I want your advice. Should we go into battle to take Ramoth-Gilead, or not?'

There was an anxious pause. Micaiah looked at the grim face of Ahab, the interested face of Jehoshaphat, and the angry faces of the four hundred prophets, who knew he was no friend of theirs. He must have felt very lonely. He laughed. 'I know the answer you want, King Ahab. Go and attack Ramoth-Gilead and the Lord will deliver it into your hand.'

The words were what Ahab wanted to hear, but the tone of voice wasn't. He was furious. He was being mocked in front of the person he most wanted to impress, King Jehoshaphat. With face red with anger he sat forward on his throne and shouted at Micaiah, 'How many times must I order you to tell me nothing except what is true in the name of the Lord?'

There was another pause. Then Micaiah spoke. His voice was different this time. It was serious, slow and sad. 'I have a vision, O king. I see the people of Israel scattered upon the hills, like sheep that have no shepherd. The Lord says these people have no master. Let them return to their houses in peace.'

The meaning of Micaiah's prophecy was painfully clear to everyone. Israel would be defeated and king Ahab himself would perish on the Syrian hills. Again rage gripped Ahab. 'What did I tell you!' he said to Jehoshaphat. 'I knew he would say something nasty about me'.

But Micaiah went on. 'Listen to the word of the Lord. I saw the Lord sitting on his throne with his heavenly host around him, and he said, "How can we persuade Ahab to attack Ramoth-Gilead so that he may fall there?" And there was much discussion. Then one of the spirits said, "I will be a lying spirit and I shall go and put lies into the mouths of his prophets, and Ahab will be persuaded." And in my vision, the Lord sent him.'

His meaning was even clearer now. Zedekiah rushed forward, beside himself with rage, and swung his fist fiercely at Micaiah, hitting him on the cheek. 'Which of your famous spirits made me do that?' he yelled angrily.

'You will understand one day,' replied Micaiah.

'Seize that man,' shouted Ahab. 'Throw him in a dungeon. Feed him on bread and water. I'll deal with him when I return victorious.'

'If you return at all,' said Micaiah as he was led away, 'The Lord has not spoken by me.' Then he turned to the bystanders. 'Hear my words, everyone of you.' Then to prison Micaiah went.

Ahab was relieved to find that the brave words of the prophet had not made Jehoshaphat change his mind about joining him in the battle. They made their preparations. Ahab, rightly suspecting that the Syrians might make him their main target, decided he would disguise himself as an ordinary soldier. However, he told Jehoshaphat to put on his kingly robes. For some reason Jehoshaphat did, and it nearly brought his downfall. The Syrians spotted him and pursued his chariot till they discovered it wasn't their old enemy, Ahab, and then they left him.

They didn't find Ahab, but a chance arrow did. He was wounded, and he died in his chariot about sunset. The day was a disaster for the Israelites, who were defeated and scattered. Jehoshaphat escaped back to Judah.

And what of Micaiah, the prophet in his dungeon? We don't know, but I like to think that Jehoshaphat went and freed him on his way back to Jerusalem.

The Beauty Queen
who saved the Jews

The news travelled through the city like wild-fire.

'Queen Vashti's disobeyed the king.'

'What do you mean?'

'She wouldn't do what he ordered.'

'At the banquet?'

'At the banquet – on the last day. The king wanted to show his queen off to all the famous people at his banquet.'

'And you say she wouldn't obey?'

'She didn't obey.'

At the palace the king was angry – very angry.

'After all,' observed one of his seven wise men, 'if the queen doesn't obey the king, all the ladies in the land will start disobeying their husbands and then . . .'

'. . . and then,' interrupted the king, 'there will be real trouble.'

The king and his seven wise men sat and thought deeply. It wasn't easy. In fact, they'd almost forgotten how to think after one hundred and eighty seven days of celebration and feasting.

'What shall I do?' asked the king.

'What you must do,' started the first wise man . . .

'. . . is issue an edict,' continued the second.

'What sort of edict?' asked the king again.

'A special edict, that can't be changed,' said the third.

'Queen Vashti must no longer be queen,' said the fourth.

The king looked worried, but said nothing.

'Another queen must be found,' advised the fifth.

'A better one,' added the sixth.

'And then,' concluded the seventh, 'all the women will have to obey their husbands.'

And that was that. An edict was issued and Queen Vashti was no longer queen. Everything seemed fine, until the king realized what he had done. In many ways, he had been rather fond of Queen Vashti, and he was sad at losing her. However, he couldn't go back on his edict, so he asked his wise men again for their advice.

'Have a beauty contest. Let your officials gather together all the girls, and then you can choose your new queen from amongst them.'

The king liked the idea, and that is what he did.

Now, in another part of the city lived two people called Mordecai and Esther. Mordecai was Esther's cousin, and he looked after her because her parents had died. They were both Jews, who had been brought to live in Susa when their own country of Judah had been invaded. Susa was the capital city of Persia, where the king lived. Esther was very beautiful, and the king's official in Susa said that she ought to go in for the beauty contest.

Mordecai and Esther talked it over, and Mordecai, who was very wise, said, 'As far as I can see, it's an excellent plan, my dear. But be sure you don't tell anyone that you are Jewish. That wouldn't be a good idea.'

A very sound piece of advice, as it turned out.

Esther went to live in the palace, and spent a whole year preparing for the contest. She did well – so well, in fact, that eveyone thought she would win – which she did. The king liked her best of all, and crowned her queen.

Very shortly after Esther had been made queen, Mordecai overheard an important conversation at the palace gates. Two of the king's guards were plotting to kill the king. He told Esther, who told the king. There was an immediate investigation and the two guards were found to be guilty. They were hanged and the king had the event written down in his special royal diary.

For the next four years Esther got on well as queen. The king loved her and she was a good queen. One person worried her, though, and that was Haman, the king's head official. He was proud and boastful, and insisted that everyone, except the king of course, was to bow down to him. However, one person always refused to bow down to him, and that was Mordecai, Esther's cousin.

'I'm a Jew,' he said, 'I don't bow down to any person except God. My religion forbids me to.'

Haman was furious. He spent a long time thinking what he could do to Mordecai, and eventually he had an idea – not a nice one at all, but a cruel and frightening idea.

'On a particular day,' he decided, 'I will kill all the Jews – Mordecai included. I'll get the king to agree to it, and organize it myself.'

He went to the king and told him that there was a

group of people in Persia, who had their own laws, who didn't obey the king, and that they ought to be got rid of. He meant the Jews, of course, although he didn't say so, and the king was completely taken in. He didn't realize just how dangerous Haman was. He told him to do what he thought was right. He even gave Haman his royal signet ring to seal the order with. Haman made his order, and saw that it was read throughout the land.

Mordecai was dismayed – as was the whole city of Susa – and immediately he went to the royal palace, and sent a message to Esther.

'You must go to the king and plead with him that he will save our people.'

Esther was frightened. Nobody was allowed to go into the king's presence unless the king called for him. To do so meant death, unless the king stretched out his golden sceptre. She told Mordecai this.

'Don't think you will escape, just because you live in the palace,' was his reply. 'You must do something. It may be that it is for this reason that you are queen.'

Esther was very scared. She hadn't seen the king for a whole month, and to do so might mean death. On the other hand, if she did nothing about it, she would probably die anyway, as a result of Haman's orders, although nobody in the palace knew that she was Jewish. She took a deep breath.

'I will go to the king,' she said slowly. 'Mordecai, you must gather together as many of our people as you can, and pray for me. I will pray too and fast

23

for three days, and then go to the king, although it is against the law, and if I die, I die.'

The three days passed slowly. Mordecai prayed with his friends. Esther prayed and fasted in the palace. When the day came, Esther put on her royal robes. It was still quite early, and all was quiet in the palace. Her footsteps rang on the marble floor as she slowly approached the king's throne room. A shiver of fear ran through her, and she felt very small, uncertain, and afraid.

'What if the king doesn't stretch out his golden sceptre?' she thought. 'What if . . .?'

She tried hard to silence the questions. By now, she was outside the throne room. Then she was in the king's presence. The king was there seated on his throne, in all his majesty. He glanced up, angry that anyone should disturb him. The sceptre in his right hand remained still.

Then he recognized Esther.

'Esther, my dear, how good to see you,' he said kindly, as he stretched out the golden sceptre towards her. 'What is it you want?'

Esther thought quickly.

'If it pleases you,' she began, 'I'd like you to come to dinner tonight – with Haman.'

'Of course,' said the king, 'We'll be there.'

And they were. The king realized that Esther wanted something rather special, so when they'd finished the meal, he asked her again.

'What is it you want? You will know I will give you whatever you want, even up to half of my kingdom.'

Esther thought again.

'I'd like you to come to dinner again,' she said. 'Tomorrow night. Yes – Haman as well.'

Haman was so pleased. Dinner with the king and queen two nights running. He went home and told his wife all about it.

'I'm a very important man,' he told her, 'Very important. The most important in all the land – except for the king, of course. He's honoured me a lot recently. More than anyone else. I've earned it, of course. Worked hard for it. And now dinner with the king and queen for two nights. What's that? Eh? – No! Nobody else going. Just me, the king and the queen.'

Then Haman remembered Mordecai.

'It's all spoilt by that Mordecai man,' he continued. 'He still refuses to bow down to me. Such a nuisance, just when everything else is going so well.'

His wife looked up.

'You could hang him, you know. On the gallows, seventy-five feet high.'

Haman looked pleased and annoyed. It was an excellent idea, but he wished he had thought of it.

'I shall tell the king to hang him tomorrow,' he said, 'before dinner.'

He had the gallows built immediately, and went to bed very satisfied.

That night the king couldn't sleep, so he asked a courtier to read to him from his royal diary. After a while, he came to the story of how Mordecai had saved the king, soon after Esther had become queen.

'Tell me,' said the king, 'have we honoured this

man, Mordecai, in any way?'

His courtier replied, 'No.'

'Well, we must. Who is here at the moment who could do something about it?'

It so happened that Haman had just arrived, in order to make arrangements with the king about hanging Mordecai.

'Send Haman here,' ordered the king.

'Tell me,' he said, when Haman arrived, 'what should I do with a man I want to honour greatly?'

'Aha!' thought Haman, 'he means me.'

'I should,' he continued out aloud, 'give him the king's royal robes, the royal crown, the royal horse, and parade him round the city, led by a courtier, calling out that here is the man the king wants to honour.'

'Excellent idea,' said the king. 'See that it's done – to Mordecai. Do the job thoroughly. Everything you mentioned.'

So Haman, very disgruntled, had to. By the time he had finished, it was dinner time.

After they had eaten, the king asked Esther again what she wanted. Esther looked at the king, then at Haman, and then back to the king.

'If it pleases you,' she began, 'I'd like the king to save my life. My life, and the lives of all my people – the Jews. We are to be killed – all of us.'

The king was horrified.

'What is this? Who is responsible for this?' he stormed.

Esther pointed at Haman, who was beginning to look rather pale. 'He is,' she said quietly.

The king was too angry to speak. He went out into the garden to cool off. When he came back, he found Haman imploring Esther to save him.

'Leave her,' shouted the king. 'Don't touch, don't even speak to my wife.'

One of the king's officials present stepped forward and said quietly to the king, 'Haman has a gallows in his garden, which he prepared for Mordecai.'

'Well, hang him then,' said the king, 'on his own gallows.'

So Haman was hanged, and his position was taken by Mordecai, who behaved wisely and sensibly. The king issued another order, cancelling Haman's order, and so Esther and her people were saved.

The story of Esther is still read by the Jews every year, on their special day called Purim, when they remember the great courage of Esther and the way in which the Jewish people were delivered.

God's Agent in Babylon

Daniel was very unhappy – mind you, he had every reason to be. He was in Babylon, hundreds of miles from his own home, Jerusalem. The King of Babylon had destroyed Jerusalem, taken him and many others captive and brought them to his own capital. What had happened to Daniel's family, he just did not know.

The king – Nebuchadnezzar was his name – thought Daniel and his friends were just the sort of people he wanted for service in the royal palace – good-looking, intelligent, knowledgeable, and ready to learn. He saw to it that they had the royal food and wine each day, and were taught the language of his country.

This made Daniel even more unhappy, because at every meal a portion of the food and wine was offered to the king's gods. Daniel was a Jew, and he worshipped the true God, and he told the king's officer this when he brought the next meal in.

'Look, I'm a Jew – my friends are too. We can't eat the royal food after it's been offered to your gods. Give us something else.'

'I can't do that,' replied the officer. 'I'm responsible to the king for you. If you started looking underfed or thin, I'd get the blame. I'd lose my head.'

'Well,' said Daniel, determined to have things his own way, 'try this. My friends and I will have vegetables to eat and water to drink for the next ten days. Then see how we look. Compare us with the others who eat the king's food.'

'All right,' said the officer, 'but I don't like it. Too risky.'

'Our God will look after us,' said Daniel confidently.

The official shrugged his shoulders, picked up the tray of royal food and left.

Ten days passed. Daniel and his friends had vegetables to eat and water to drink for all their meals – not very exciting, but to them it was far better than eating food which had been offered to the king's gods. What is more, at the end of the ten days, they looked more healthy than any of the others who had fed on the royal food.

The officer agreed grudgingly. 'All right,' he said, 'we'll keep it this way. I hope your God continues to look after you, for my sake.'

And of course, he did. Daniel and his friends had honoured God, so God honoured them. He saw to it that they were wiser than all the other wise men in the kingdom. In fact, whenever the king asked for their advice, he found them ten times better than anyone else.

Some time later, Nebuchadnezzar had a dream. As is the way so often with dreams, he couldn't remember anything about it. All he knew was that he'd had a dream, and that it was an important one. He couldn't sleep any more that night, so as soon as it was light, he called his wise men together. They came rushing to the palace, rather bleary-eyed, and a little annoyed at being woken so early.

'Tell me my dream,' demanded Nebuchadnezzar.

The wise men looked at one another, dumb-founded.

'If you please, O king,' they said, 'You must tell us your dream. Then we will tell you what it means.'

'If you can tell the future from dreams,' thundered the king, 'you can tell the past. What was my dream? Tell me, and I reward you. Fail, and you die.'

But they couldn't tell the king, so he commanded that they be killed.

Now Daniel got to hear of these events, and one thing that Daniel was very good at was under-standing dreams. He plucked up courage and went to the king immediately, asking him to save the wise men, and also give him a while in order to find out the dream.

The king agreed, and Daniel went back to his friends.

'Look,' he said, 'the king has had a dream' – and he told them the matter. 'We must pray to God, who I'm sure will tell us the dream and its meaning.'

And God did – during the night. Daniel was very thankful. If he had not been able to tell the king his dream in the morning, he and his friends would have perished with the wise men.

He went straight to the palace, and was shown into the king's presence.

'Ah!' said the king, 'Here you are. Well, can you tell me the dream?'

'I can't,' said Daniel, 'Nobody could – but there is a God in heaven who reveals secrets, and he has shown me the dream.'

'Go on – tell me the dream,' said the king impatiently.

'In your dream, O king,' explained Daniel, 'You saw a great statue made of gold, silver, bronze, iron and clay, and this great statue was smashed by a stone which gradually became a mountain.'

King Nebuchadnezzar smiled. It was all coming back to him now. But what did it all mean? Daniel had the answer ready.

'The statue,' he went on, 'means the great empires of the world. Your empire, O king, is the greatest, and the empires after yours are less powerful. Eventually all these will be destroyed and replaced by God's empire, which will become greater than any other.'

Daniel's courage and faith were rewarded. The king was very pleased. He praised Daniel's God, and honoured Daniel by making him ruler of the province of Babylon, and chief of the wise men. Later, the king began to serve and worship Daniel's God.

Time passed, and eventually he died. Belshazzar was made king, and one day, he decided to give a feast for a thousand of his lords.

'A grand feast,' he said, 'to show how grand Babylon is.'

A strange thing to say, because at that very time, a foreign army was besieging Babylon, and Babylon's defeat was very near.

'We'll use the Jewish temple flagons,' he went on, 'just to show that our gods are greater than theirs.'

He had no thought for the poor in his city, half-starved because of the siege.

'We'll praise our gods, we'll eat and drink as never before.'

And that's what they did, late into the night, while the foreign army changed the course of the river Euphrates that flowed through the city, and started to invade Babylon along the dry river bed.

The feasting was at its height. There was shouting, singing and laughter. The foreign army was forgotten. Everyone was very merry – when suddenly, on the large white wall of the feasting room, appeared the fingers of a man's hand. The king saw it first. He turned pale, and his knees started to knock together. Gradually a stunned silence spread across the room. The gold and silver drinking vessels clattered to the floor. What did it all mean?

Then the hand started to move. It wrote four words – four words which no-one present could read – and then disappeared. But the words remained.

Belshazzar broke the silence.

'Well,' he almost screamed, 'what is it? What does it mean?'

But no one knew.

'Bring the wise men in,' he stormed. 'The person who reads this shall be the third most important person in my kingdom.'

But the wise men didn't know what the writing meant.

The king was very pale, and utterly dismayed. His wife came to the rescue. She had heard about Daniel and his understanding of dreams, and she told

Belshazzar. He frowned. He didn't get on with Daniel too well. But his wife was persistent.

'Call him,' she said. 'He'll tell you what the words mean.'

She was right. Daniel knew what the words meant the moment he entered the room. He also knew about the invading army. But to tell the king was another matter completely.

'Tell me,' demanded the king. 'Tell me. Quickly!'

Daniel took a deep breath.

'O King Belshazzar', he started, 'all this has happenned because you have not honoured the true God.'

The king looked annoyed, but he didn't say anything. Daniel continued.

'You have dishonoured the true God by using these drinking vessels from the Jewish temple. You have worshipped your own false gods. You have ignored the true God. He wrote this writing, and this is what it means. God has brought your kingdom to its end. You have failed in your rule. Your kingdom has been given to the invading army.'

He stopped, wondering what the king's reaction would be. He could be hanged for these words, if the mood took the king that way. But Belshazzar had made a promise, and he had to stick to it.

'Bring a purple robe,' he commanded. 'Put a gold chain round his neck. He shall be the third most important person in the land.'

Obviously, the full meaning of Daniel's words had not yet sunk in.

Later that night, the invading army conquered

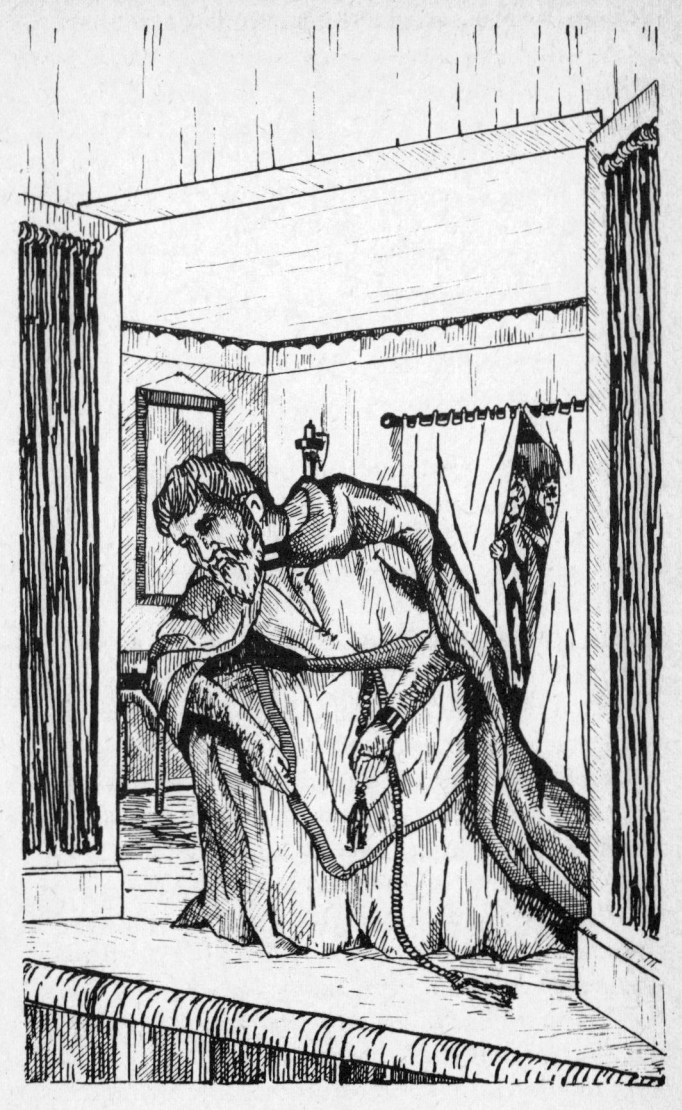

Babylon, and Belshazzar was killed.

The new king was Darius and he liked Daniel. In fact, Daniel did so well that Darius wanted to make him ruler over the whole kingdom. Of course, many of the other governors and officials were very jealous, and they got together to think up a way to find fault with Daniel.

'There's no way we can do it,' they decided, 'unless we find something wrong with his religion and the God he worships.'

So they went to King Darius.

'O King Darius, may you live for ever,' they started. Then they got down to the point. 'We all think, O king, that for the next thirty days, no one should pray to any god, except to you.'

King Darius was rather flattered.

'If anyone does,' they went on, 'he should be thrown straight into the pit of lions. Here's the law. Please sign it, King Darius.'

And King Darius, completely taken in, did so.

The governors hurried off, delighted that their plan was going so well. Now all they had to do was to catch Daniel praying to his God.

Daniel was no coward. He had always prayed to his God, and this new Law, which he knew all about, certainly wasn't going to stop him. He went straight up to his room, opened the window which faced towards his home, and prayed to his God – three times a day – as he had always done before.

Of course, it was easy for the governors and officials to find him. Off they ran, back to King Darius.

'You did sign that law, didn't you, O king?'

'It is signed, and nothing can change it now,' agreed the king.

'Well, we've found somebody breaking it already,' they said. 'It's that Daniel man. He pays no attention to you, O king. In fact, he prays to his God three times a day.'

Darius was very upset. He hadn't seen how this law was going to work out. For the rest of that day, he tried to think how to save Daniel, but he couldn't.

Then the governors and officials came back.

'You can't change the law, O king,' and King Darius knew that he would have to throw Daniel into the lions' pit.

Daniel was arrested. Just before the guards threw him into the pit, the king took him aside.

'May your own God, whom you pray to, save you, Daniel.'

The king returned to his palace, very distressed. He had no supper, and he went straight to bed. He didn't sleep, but worried all night about Daniel. As soon as it was light, he hurried back to the lions' pit.

'Surely,' he thought, 'there's no chance of . . . .'

But there was. As he approached the pit, Daniel called out 'O king, my God has saved me. His messenger shut the lions' mouths, and they haven't hurt me at all.'

King Darius was overjoyed. He commanded that Daniel should be set free, and he made another law.

'All people in my kingdom,' he declared, 'are to honour and worship Daniel's God, for he is great.

A Disciple on Trial

One sunny afternoon, as Peter and John walked up the streets of Jerusalem towards the great, glittering Temple building, they noticed ahead of them two men, carrying another man on his mattress. As they got closer to the entrance to the Temple, they began to catch them up and then they could see who it was. It was the old lame beggar, who always sat just beside the gate. He was there every day, hoping that people going into the Temple would throw a coin into his begging bowl.

By the time they had reached the outer court of the Temple, Peter and John were quite close to the beggar, and at that moment he looked up and saw them.

'Money for the lame beggar,' he shouted in a loud, whining voice. He was not going to miss any chance.

'I'm afraid we haven't any money,' said Peter and, as he said it, he could see disappointment come into the man's face. 'But there is something we can give you.' The beggar looked a little more cheerful, but also rather puzzled. 'In the name of Jesus Christ, walk.'

The two people carrying him stopped, and everybody nearby pressed in as close as they could, to see what would happen. They put the mattress on the ground. The lame man felt his legs, he stretched them, wriggled them and got on to his knees. Peter

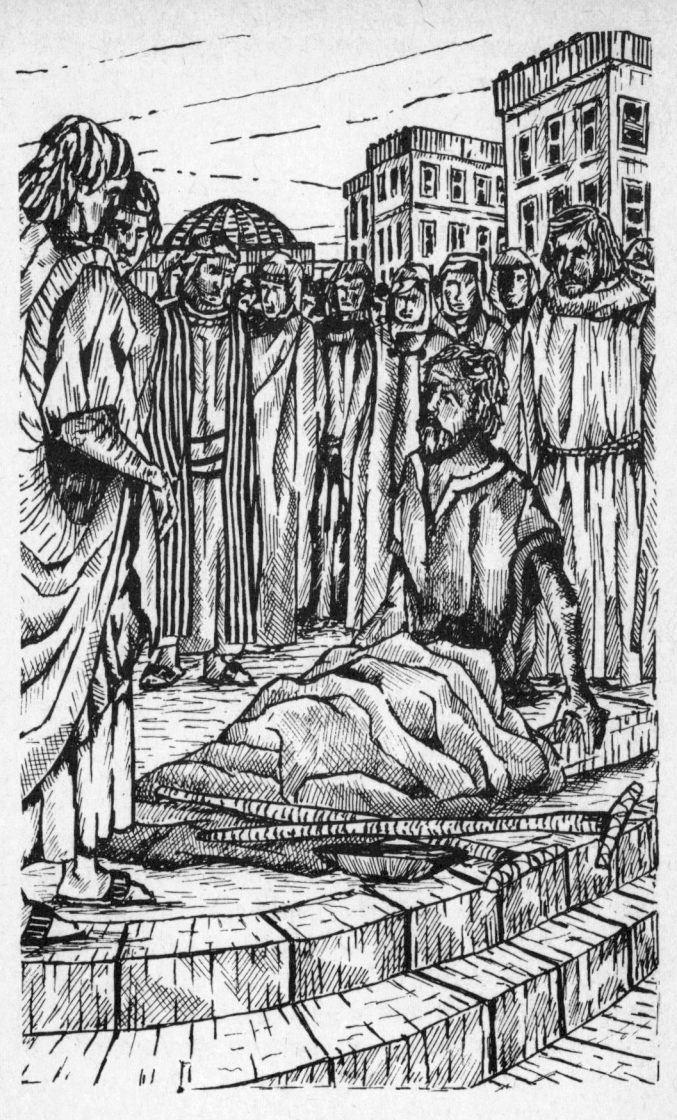

seized his arm and heaved him to his feet. Gingerly, he put one foot in front of another. Then Peter let go, and he took a few steps all on his own. Suddenly he gave a jump in the air.

'I can walk. I can walk,' he shouted. 'I'm all right again. Thank you, thank you!' he said to Peter and John.

'Don't thank us,' said Peter. 'Thank God. He's the one who has done it.'

As the lame man tried out his legs, and jumped and ran and shouted out thanks to God, the news began to spread through the Temple court. Everyone was amazed to see the old beggar walking around, and soon a huge crowd gathered to see the people who had done the miracle. This seemed a golden opportunity to Peter to tell all these people about Jesus. He did not stop to worry about what the rulers might think about it.

'Listen,' he said. 'You all remember this beggar here who used to sit every day beside the gate. And you can see he has been made better. Well, we're not the ones who've done it. It is God the Father of the Lord Jesus who healed him.'

'Jesus?' asked some of the people in the crowd. 'We thought he was dead.'

'Yes, Jesus,' said Peter, 'the man you killed on the cross. You thought you'd rather let that wicked murderer Barabbas live and kill the Son of God in his place. But God has brought Jesus back from the dead.' Peter went on to explain how they could have new life in Jesus.

Most of the crowd listened hard, and wanted

Peter to go on and tell them more. But there were just a few who felt very angry about what was going on and what Peter was saying. These people were the Pharisees – the main people who had killed Jesus. They had hated Jesus, and they also hated anyone who followed him. They were not going to allow Peter to preach freely in the Temple, of all places. Quietly, one or two of them slipped away from the crowd and up through the temple to fetch some of the temple guards.

Meanwhile Peter went on preaching, but a few minutes later, he heard the tramp of soldiers' feet. Soon a group of priests and guards appeared and came straight towards Peter and John in the centre of the crowd. They quickly and roughly grabbed hold of Peter and John by the arms. There was nothing anyone could do. While the temple guards dragged Peter and John away, and the long evening shadows darkened the Temple court, the crowd slowly drifted towards home, thinking about what Peter had said and what had happened. Many of them decided to follow Jesus because of what they had heard.

Peter and John found themselves in a part of the Temple they had never seen before. They had to go down a long corridor in which the guards' footsteps echoed loudly. Finally, they came to a door with huge metal bolts on the outside. The leader of the guards pulled back the bolts with a clang, and then pushed Peter and John into a small, dark room, shut the door and snapped the bolts back into place.

For a moment, as they lay on the hard stone floor

of their cell, they felt depressed and miserable. They had had such a wonderful afternoon, with Jesus healing the lame man and the chance to preach to all those people, and now here they were in prison, not knowing whether they would ever get out of it alive. Peter felt a sickening fear inside, and he could not help thinking back to what had happened a few months before.

He remembered how he had said so confidently to Jesus, 'Whatever anyone else does, I'll never leave you. I'll even die for you.' Then a few hours later, when the soldiers had come in the darkness to capture Jesus, Peter had not stood by him but had crept along behind in the shadows. Next came the most painful moment to remember. He had gone into the High Priest's house to see what would happen, and in the flickering light at the doorway, the doorkeeper had recognized him and asked him if he was one of Jesus's disciples. 'No!' Peter had said angrily. Twice more, round the fire in the courtyard, people had asked him the same question, and each time, angrier still, he had said, 'No!' Then Peter remembered how Jesus had turned to look at him. The cock had crowed and he had rushed blindly outside, crying with shame.

As he thought about the past, Peter remembered, too, that it had all happened before he had understood properly the point of Jesus's life. Since that dreadful day, a change had come over him. Jesus himself was living in him now and Jesus would give him courage to face the trouble they were in. He and John talked about this together for a while and, when they had made themselves as comfortable as they could, they peacefully went to sleep till morning.

When the light of day began to creep into their cell, they soon woke up and began to think about the things that might happen to them that day. They prayed together about it, and Peter asked God particularly to give him courage to stand up for what they believed, whatever the priests and Pharisees did to them. Before very long, they heard the bolts rattling and one of the guards threw some food into the room. They had only just finished eating it when the guard appeared again: 'Get up and come with me,' he commanded. 'Come on, hurry up. The council is waiting to give you your trial.'

The guards surrounded them and marched them down the corridor, out through the Temple courts and in through the great doors of the council chamber. The priests sat in a great semi-circle and, as Peter and John came in, they were whispering together. When everyone was in place. the High Priest stood up. His face was red with anger. 'What right have you to do these things and almost cause a riot in the Temple courts!' he shouted.

Peter needed all the courage that Jesus could give him to answer boldly now. 'Gentlemen, if you are worried about how the old lame beggar was healed,' he said calmly, 'Then I'll explain. It is Jesus, the man you people murdered –' the priests and Pharisees muttered angrily – 'the man God has brought back to life – his power healed the cripple. And what's more, you ought to know that there is no other way of getting to know God and having your sins forgiven except through him.' No one could have guessed that this Peter was the same one who had only a few months before betrayed Jesus three times. All the priests had to sit round in their long robes and grey beards and listen while Peter preached to them about Jesus. They became more and more furious, and longed to hear a really harsh punishment given to Peter and John.

The High Priest was very angry indeed, too, and he was just as keen to punish them, but just as he was going to speak, he noticed something – the old cripple who had been healed was standing in the room, too, for everyone to see. There did not seem to be any doubt that he really had been healed. That made things very awkward. He knew what the crowd would think if he punished the men who had healed the cripple. That really might cause a riot. The High Priest thought quickly. They would have to decide what to do. 'Take these men out,' he ordered. The Council wish to discuss the case.'

'Out you go!' said the warder, and prodded his two prisoners out into the corridor and along to a small room. 'Sit in there,' he said. 'And don't try anything because I shall be waiting outside.' Peter and John waited while the priests discussed inside, and a crowd gathered to find out what was happening to their heroes.

'We can't have them killed,' explained the High Priest. 'The crowd wouldn't stand for it. We shall have to think of something else.'

A tall Pharisee with a thin face and hooked nose

stood up. 'We must whip them at least to teach them a lesson. We can't allow low-class fellows like these to tell us what to do.'

'I am afraid the crowd would cause trouble if we even did that,' a short, plump priest pointed out.

'You are quite right, Ephraim,' said the High Priest. 'All we can do is make sure they do not continue to go around preaching.' He looked round at the angry faces and then said, 'Bring back the prisoners.' A guard scurried out to fetch Peter and John.

When they were standing in front of the council again, the High Priest stood up once more, gathering his robes about him, and said very solemnly, 'We have decided not to punish you this time, but you must promise never to preach about this Jesus person again. As long as you promise this you will go free.' The old Peter who had betrayed Jesus would have been glad to promise and get away with his life. The new Peter with the spirit of Jesus answered boldly, 'Which would you rather we did, obey you or God? God has told us to preach about Jesus and we'll go on doing that whatever you or any other man tells us to do.' The whole Council seethed with fury as they listened to this, but they were too afraid of the crowd to do anything about it.

'We warn you that you will be punished if you continue to do this,' threatened the High Priest. When this had no effect, he had no choice but to say at last, 'Guards, take these men out and let them go.'

The Prisoners Who Would Not Escape

Once Paul was in Philippi, a city in Northern Greece. It was the first time that he had been there, and Paul was hoping that he would be able to make friends with the local people. With him were his friends Luke, Timothy and Silas. The four of them stayed in Philippi for some time, and one day they decided to go down to the river, outside the city gate. Here a small group of people used to meet together for prayer. Before very long Paul and Silas were talking to the people. Paul told them that Jesus was alive and that if they trusted in him, he would forgive their sins. 'Listen,' said Paul. 'Not long ago I didn't believe in this Jesus of Nazareth. In fact I did all I could to hunt down his followers and put them in prison. Then, while I was going to Damascus to arrest some of these disciples of Jesus, a very strange thing happened.' Paul stopped talking and looked round at the interested faces of the people.

'Go on,' said a lady named Lydia, who seemed to be the leader of the group. 'What happened next?'

Paul carried on with his story. 'I was walking along the road when suddenly a very bright light shone down from the sky. It was so bright it blinded me. I fell down on to the road and heard someone talking to me. I'm sure it was Jesus speaking.'

'Then what happened?' asked one of the men.

'Well, to cut a long story short, I realized that I'd

been doing wrong. Now, instead of arresting disciples, I tell people all about Jesus, the Son of God. Jesus is alive and if you trust in him, he will forgive you your sins. In other words, he will forgive you for all the wrong things you've ever done. This is really true. I should know – not long ago I was a sinner, but now Jesus has forgiven me.'

Lydia was so impressed by what Paul had said that she asked if she could be baptized. This would be a sign to the people that she had come to believe in Jesus. Lydia also insisted that Paul and his friends should go and stay at her home.

While they were staying with Lydia, Paul and the others often used to wander around the city streets, and walk along by the side of the river. Paul told the people about the Lord Jesus. Soon everyone knew the four men who had come to Philippi with this new teaching.

Since becoming a follower of Jesus, Paul found that he had made quite a lot of enemies. What would happen if they caught him? Once he had been stoned and left nearly dead. What would they do if they ever caught him again? Would they beat him or put him in prison, stone him or even kill him? Paul knew he was risking his life by going on preaching, but he still carried on. The people had to be told the good news about Jesus, the Son of God. This was what God wanted Paul to do.

One day, as Paul and his friends were walking towards the river, they saw a poor slave girl. The girl had an evil spirit inside her, and she earned her wicked owners a lot of money by telling people's fortunes. She followed Paul and the others, shouting, 'These men are servants of the Most High God! They will tell you what you must do if you want to go to Heaven!' Many people stopped what they were doing and turned to look at the slave girl and then at Paul and his three friends. What did the girl mean?

This went on for some days and at last Paul's patience was exhausted. It was time he put a stop to this. Not caring what the people would think, Paul turned round and stared at the girl. Then he spoke to the evil spirit inside her. 'I order you in the name of Jesus Christ to come out of that poor girl.' All at once the evil spirit left her, and she became a normal person again. Now she could no longer tell people's fortunes.

Paul looked at the crowd of people surrounding him. Everyone was very quiet. They could hardly believe what had happened. But the silence was soon broken. There were angry shouts from the girl's owners. They were furious with Paul, because now that the girl couldn't tell any more fortunes, they would not be able to use her to make them any more money. The men came up to Paul and Silas, as the leaders of the group, grabbed them, and dragged them along the street to the market place. Before long, Paul and Silas were facing the local magistrates. 'These men are causing trouble in the city. They are breaking our laws, and trying to get the people to believe in the teachings of Jesus of Nazareth!' The crowd shouted out in agreement. 'Yes,' they cried, 'These men have caused nothing but trouble since they arrived at Philippi. It's time someone dealt with them. Beat them both!'

'We're in real trouble now,' whispered Paul, and Silas nodded his head.

The magistrates didn't give the two men a chance to prove their innocence. 'Strip them,' said the magistrates, and the clothes were ripped from off the backs of Paul and Silas. The crowd started to cheer. The two trouble-makers were going to be beaten. That would teach them to go round upsetting people with all their talk about this Jesus of Nazareth. Everyone watched as Paul and Silas were beaten until their backs were red with blood.

That wasn't the end of their punishment. As soon as the beating was over, one of the magistrates said, 'Now put these men in prison, and make sure they're kept well locked up. That should keep them out of trouble!' The magistrates handed over Paul and Silas to the governor of the city prison, and the two friends were taken away.

They soon arrived at the prison. A jailer led Paul and Silas to one of the deepest dungeons and clapped their legs into the stocks. The two men were left in darkness. Beaten, and then put in prison – what a day it had been!

Slowly their eyes grew accustomed to the dim light and they looked around the dungeon. What a place! They could hear the groaning of the other prisoners, and they knew that as faithful followers of Jesus Christ they would have a fairly tough time in prison. Paul tried to go to sleep, but he couldn't. His back was far too sore.

As he sat in the darkness, Paul thought over the

events of the last few days. Since his strange experience on his way to Damascus, Paul was sure he was doing right by telling as many people as possible that Jesus really did forgive sinners. If this was the job God had given Paul to do, then he wanted to do it, no matter how difficult it was. So, instead of complaining, Paul and Silas started to pray. They asked God to be with them, and watch over them. Then, to the amazement of the other prisoners, they began singing hymns. They carried on singing until it was almost midnight.

Suddenly there was a strange noise, and the earth began to shake. There was a rumbling sound, then another, and then there was a crashing noise. Some of the other prisoners began to cry out in fright. Paul looked at Silas. What was happening now? It sounded very like an earthquake. There was another terrific rumbling noise, the ground shook, and the prison walls started to collapse. Then the doors flew open. The stocks were shattered, and the chains came away from the walls. The prisoners were free. Paul and Silas leapt to their feet but, instead of escaping, Paul shouted out, 'Do not escape! Stay just where you are!' The other prisoners thought Paul was mad. This was their chance to get away. They moved towards Paul and Silas. 'No!' shouted Paul. 'We must stay here!'

When the jailer woke up, he saw at once that the prison doors were wide open, and he thought that all the prisoners must have escaped. This meant that the authorities would probably kill him for allowing Paul and Silas to get away. So he decided to kill

himself. He drew his sword. Paul, from the darkness of the dungeon, saw that the jailer was going to commit suicide. 'Do not harm yourself!' he shouted. 'We are all here.' Quickly the jailer got some lights, and he rushed into the dungeon. Trembling with fear, he fell down in front of Paul and Silas. Then he led the prisoners outside and said, 'Sirs, oh sirs, what must I do to be saved?'

'Believe in the Lord Jesus,' replied Paul. 'Then you will be saved, you and your family.'

Paul knew that the jailer and his family would not really understand what he meant, so he told them more about Jesus. Although it was still the middle of the night, the jailer got some water and washed the backs of Paul and Silas, and later he and his family were baptized. Paul and Silas were taken to the jailer's house and given food and drink.

Next morning some men came to the prison. They said that the magistrates had decided to release the two prisoners. The jailer told Paul the good news. 'The magistrates have decided to release you. You're free men.' But Paul was annoyed. 'We're Roman citizens,' he said. 'We've been beaten in front of all the people in the market place, and then thrown into prison without a trial. Now they want us to go away secretly. No, certainly not! The magistrates must come and take us out of the prison themselves!'

Sure enough, before long, the magistrates arrived and apologized to Paul and Silas for the way they had been treated. The magistrates led the two friends out of the prison and asked them to leave the city.

Paul and Silas were free! At once they went to

Lydia's house, where they found Luke and Timothy. Paul explained what had happened, and that he and Silas had to leave the city.

While Lydia was getting them food for their journey, Paul talked to some of the Philippian Christians. 'Listen,' he said. 'I've got to go away, so now you must carry on telling people the good news about the Lord Jesus. It won't always be easy, but don't give up as soon as things start to go wrong!'

Paul and Silas said goodbye to Lydia, Timothy, and Luke, and set off on their journey. Soon Philippi was left far behind them.

Paul didn't forget all about his friends in Philippi. He often prayed for them, and he wrote them letters to see how they were getting on. Later, he may have actually returned to Philippi. The Philippians showed their love for Paul by sending him help when he was in prison later in his life.

Kidnapped for Slavery

Patrick lay back on the rather damp grass, shut his eyes and let the sun warm him all over like a joint in an oven. 'Some sunshine at last,' he thought. 'It's been raining for weeks.' All around him were the Irish hills. They were covered with patches of purple heather and with grass which was a deep green from the rain and kept short by the sheep Patrick was looking after. A sheep bleated close by and made him jump, but otherwise everything was quiet and peaceful.

As he lay back, Patrick could not help thinking about home in England, about his parents and friends away across the water of the Irish Sea. It was six years since he had seen them last. He thought back to that dreadful night six years ago. In his mind he could see himself; he was lying in bed asleep, snuggled down in the darkness. Suddenly something woke him. There was a noise of shouting. A flaring torch entered the room. He tried to shield his eyes, but a great black-bearded face bent over him and with one huge hairy arm, he was heaved out of bed.

'Get your clothes on,' the bearded man said. 'You're coming with us!'

'Why? What's happening?'

'Just do as you're told, and you won't be harmed. Try to get away and then . . .' Patrick saw a spear glint in the torchlight.

On the peaceful hillside, Patrick opened his eyes and shook his head to try to get rid of the horrible picture in his mind. But he could not help remembering the journey that came afterwards. The raiders had driven a large group of captives, including Patrick, into their little open boats. He remembered how seasick he had felt when the boat leapt on the waves like a frightened horse. After the voyage had come the slave market, and he discovered why they had captured him. Although he was exhausted, he had to stand for hours in the market while great rough chieftains and wealthy farmers pushed and poked him and felt his muscles, until one of them, Miliucc, decided to buy him to work as a shepherd.

And that was how he came to be lying out in the sunshine on the grass. One good thing had come out of all this trouble, though. Patrick had really come to know God. In England, his parents had told him a lot about God but he had not taken much notice. All on his own in the Irish hills, Patrick discovered that God was a real person he could talk to. And he certainly needed a friend.

A few days later, he made up his mind to try to get home to see his parents. It would be very difficult. He would have to escape from his master, get across Ireland to the shore without being captured, and then cross the Irish Sea to reach England again. It seemed almost impossible, but as Patrick talked to God each day, he came to feel sure that God would help him. Even so, he felt very afraid as he thought about what might happen to him – a runaway slave would not stand much chance if he were caught. But he found that as he became more certain that this was what God wanted him to do, so he found he had more courage to do it.

Next day, as dawn began to break, Patrick slipped out of the house of his master for the last time. He carried a little food and his belongings in a bundle. As he went through the yard, the dogs yapped loudly. He froze and could hear his heart thumping but, fortunately, no one stirred. Soon he was standing, panting a little, on the hills where he had looked after the sheep. He looked back down to the tiny speck which was the farmhouse where he had lived for six years. He could not help feeling a little sad at leaving it.

It was a hard journey to the sea. Often Patrick wished he had not started out and felt like giving up, but somehow God gave him the courage to keep going. At last, he arrived at a hill from which he could see the blue Irish Sea stretching towards England and hear the sound of the breakers on the shore. He walked down to the beach and, as he walked, he realized that the next bit was going to be the most difficult part of the journey.

Down at the quayside, he looked to see what ships there were. Quite a few were tied up there.

'Where are you going?' he asked the sailors on a small sailing boat.

'Oh, we're heading for Gaul,' they replied.

That was no good. He tried one after another until at last he found one heading for England. Now the problem was to persuade the captain to take him.

'What is your cargo?' he asked a seaman.

'Irish wolf hounds.'

'Do you need anyone to help look after them?'

'I don't know. You'd do best to ask the captain.'

'Where is he? Can I see him?' The seaman looked down into the ship 'Captain, there's a lad here wants to speak to you.'

A burly, bearded sailor appeared and asked roughly, 'Well, what do you want?'

'I'm trying to get to England and . . . .'

'If you've got gold to pay for it, then maybe –' said the captain.

'No, I haven't any money. I thought perhaps I could help look after the cargo and work my passage.'

The captain shook his head. 'I'm sorry, mate, I've got all the men I need. I can't take any more. Now, get out of the way – we're busy.'

Patrick turned away, feeling utterly miserable. He had come all this distance and through so many difficulties and now there was no way of crossing the sea. It was hopeless. He began to think that God, his friend, had let him down. What could he do now? As he wandered slowly away from the shore, he begged God to sort things out and to get him across the sea somehow.

Suddenly, he heard footsteps behind him. Perhaps someone was chasing him. He speeded up. Then came a shout. 'Hey, wait a minute!' Patrick turned round. It was one of the sailors. What could he want? The sailor panted up to him. 'My, I had a job to catch you. You certainly walk fast.'

'What do you want?' asked Patrick still rather

frightened.

'The captain's changed his mind. He'll take you on board after all. He has found out that he'll need an extra helper.'

'Oh, thank you!' Patrick practically shouted. God had answered his prayer and would take him home.

That evening, Patrick went aboard and, after a long voyage, he reached England. Soon he was almost home. There it was – he could see the house down in the valley. The lights were shining. Patrick ran down the slope and up to the door. He hammered on it. It opened and there was his father.

'Who do you think you are, knocking so late in the evening?' he said.

'It's me, Dad!' said Patrick. 'Don't you recognize me?' Suddenly, Patrick's father realized who it was.

'Patrick, my son,' he said quietly. 'We didn't think you'd ever come back.... Mother, come and see who's here!'

It was a happy family that sat down to supper that evening. Patrick's parents were very glad that he had come back, and he was thankful to God that he had helped him through all that long journey home. Patrick remained with his parents for quite a long time, but after a while he found that God wanted him to go back to the place which he had hated so much at first. Although he would much rather have stayed in England, he went to Ireland again to preach about Jesus to the Irish. He knew that was what God wanted him to do. He was never afraid to tell people about Jesus, and this led to many adventures.

One day he visited a king. Some of the king's guards allowed him and a few friends to go into the hall, a large wooden building. The guards pushed him forward to stand in front of the king. The king was tall, had black hair bound with a golden ring, and wore a dark green tunic and a long purple cloak. Patrick and his friends knelt down and held out a present they had brought.

'Well then, what have you to say?' the king demanded as he took their present.

'I come in the name of Jesus Christ,' said Patrick, 'to tell you that the one and only Lord God has sent his Son . . .' As he spoke those words, Patrick felt a hand close over his mouth from behind. He felt the jab of a spear in his back. He tried to shout, but could not. Two soldiers were firmly holding him and pushing him out of the hall, along a corridor and then to some steps which went down into the ground. With each step down, the light grew fainter and the air damper and colder. When he reached the bottom, the guard gave a push and sent Patrick sprawling on to the mud floor of their prison. Soon Patrick's friends landed in a heap on the floor too. And there they had to sit in pitch darkness, feeling very scared and wondering what was going to happen to them. Outside the thick wooden door, they could hear the guards stamping to keep warm and chatting amongst themselves.

'Well, that lot won't have long to wait,' said one.

'No,' they heard another voice say. 'Nobody lives for long once they go in there.'

The last hope for Patrick and his friends seemed

to have gone. It was tempting to panic – to blame God. Patrick tried to pray: 'Please give me courage. If You want me to die, help me to die bravely for the sake of Jesus.' They all did their best to encourage each other but it was difficult not to feel depressed. From time to time they heard footsteps. They listened silently and their hearts strained inside them as they wondered whether it was the guards coming to take them away to execution.

Slowly, the hours passed. They sang hymns to keep their spirits up and Patrick prayed aloud. The night passed and a new day came. A little light crept into the prison, enough to see the damp glistening on the walls, to see their own filthy, haggard faces. A little food was thrown down the steps. They ate hungrily. Still they waited but no one came, nothing happened. They prayed to God that he would get them out of prison unless it was his will that they should die.

Days passed. Soon they had been there over a week and still had no idea what would happen to them. Then one morning they heard the footsteps of several men coming nearer and nearer. Again they wondered if they were going to die. The steps stopped outside the door. A guard flung open the door with a great clang.

'Come out!' he shouted. Nervously Patrick and his friends climbed the steps. When they reached the top, the guard told them gruffly, 'The king has decided to pardon you. You will be able to go. Follow me!' He turned and marched off heavily down the passage and the prisoners followed hardly daring to believe what they had heard. Soon they were out in the open again. They took deep breaths of the fresh air. They felt overjoyed to be in daylight and to see the sky, sun, grass and trees once more. They thanked God there and then for setting them free.

What they had gone through would be enough to put most people off ever preaching again for the rest of their lives. But Patrick was not put off. Instead, he went on preaching throughout Ireland for many more years.

One story tells of how he visited a place called Tara at Easter time. Despite the anger of the High-King, he climbed the hill of Slane and there he and his followers made a huge pile of sticks and logs. Watching them with ever growing fury were the Druids, the pagan priests of the land. They were men who were afraid that they would lose their great power if people became Christians. They were determined to prevent Patrick from preaching if they possibly could. As the pile of sticks grew higher, their chanting and screaming of spells and curses grew louder like a wind rising in the trees.

Suddenly there was a crackle and a roar. The fire had been lit and was sending a wing of red flame tipped with sparks soaring into the sky. Patrick climbed up on to a rock and everyone – the Druids, too – turned to look at him as he began to speak.

'I have come to tell you,' he said, 'that the Son of God, Jesus Christ, has come into the world. Evil men killed him – but he has come back to life again. Not only that, but he is alive now!' As he said those words, the fire burst upwards, red and golden, and the Druids fell silent. They could feel the power of God speaking through Patrick.

Later that evening, in the hall of the king, Patrick went on to explain to the king and all his men what being a Christian meant. This time there was no prison for Patrick. Rather, he was overjoyed to see a great number of people coming to believe in Jesus.

Other stories are told about Patrick; about the chiefs who hated him and those who loved him. But whatever happened, he did not lose either his trust in God or his great courage. Right up to the end of his life, he went on preaching and through him many thousands of Irish people became Christians.

Saved from the Flames

Fire broke out in the thatched roof of an old rectory in Lincolnshire. The flames spread quickly to the rest of the house. The noise woke the rector and his wife. They dashed from room to room to rescue their large family. The girls were able to hurry down the staircase themselves and, choking with smoke and crying with fright, they dashed out into the garden. Their mother soon followed, carrying baby Charles in her arms. Then came the father. Though the house burned and crackled behind him, he was happy because he thought his whole family was safe. 'Let the house go,' he said to the crowd who had gathered. But he was wrong. He thought his eldest boy, John, was in the garden, but John was still up in his attic bedroom.

John's face suddenly appeared at the window. There was a gasp from the crowd. The rector tried to dash back into the house, but the wooden staircase had collapsed and the flames and smoke drove him back.

'Quick, a ladder,' shouted someone.

'There's no time for that,' came a reply. 'I'll stand against the wall of the house. Climb on my shoulders.'

Up the man jumped. He was tall, and leaning against the wall which was now hot from the flames, he stretched his arms towards the attic window. The six-year-old boy half-jumped and half-slithered into them. Strong hands caught him. He was safe.

This boy was John Wesley, who was going to grow up to be one of the most famous men in England. When he was older, he described his rescue from the flames as a miracle of God. He felt sure that God had rescued him and that God must have some important job for him to do.

God had. The job was to tell all the people of Britain the good news of Jesus Christ. John became a clergyman like his father, but he did not preach his sermons in quiet, comfortable churches, but somewhere quite new in those days – outside. He spoke in market places, factory yards or on village greens – anywhere where people would come and listen.

To do this, John travelled a quarter of a million miles, usually on horseback. Most of the roads in those days would seem like farm tracks to us. Many towns and villages were cut off from the outside world after heavy rains by a sea of mud, but neither mud nor rains nor storms ever stopped John Wesley. He was up at four every morning for prayer and Bible study. Often he was on the road before six. And he must have been a good rider, or good at training his horses, because often he was seen riding along reading a book!

Many people, especially the poor, were glad to hear him. This was why he preached outside, because the churches had become sleepy, with boring sermons from clergymen who preferred hunting foxes and drinking with the squire to mixing with the poor. Inside the churches the working folk in their old clothes felt out of place and unwanted. But John Wesley went to them, and told them they were wanted – by Jesus. Many responded gladly but there were also many who were against him.

Drunkards screamed insults at him. Often men and boys threw mud and stones and rotten vegetables at him. Once a herd of cows was driven into his congregation on a village green. There was confusion and some stone-throwing. He was hit between the eyes. It was painful; he felt stunned. But his audience were on his side. With angry shouts they drove the poor cows and the stone throwers away. John wiped away the blood from his forehead and told them to take courage, for God had not given the spirit of fear.

Another time it was a bull that was used to break up John's meeting. He was speaking from an old wooden table, when an angry bull was loosed in his direction. The terrified crowd parted as the bull headed straight for the table. John went on talking, and the bull swerved aside at the last moment. As the bull charged into the distance, John was still talking. It would take more than an angry bull to stop him.

Perhaps his most frightening experience was in Darlaston in Staffordshire, where an angry crowd surrounded the house in which he was staying. Fierce-looking men called for him to come out. John asked their leaders to come in, and spoke calmly with them. Then he went out and faced the whole crowd. He called for a chair and began to speak. Just as all seemed to be going well another

gang from the next town, Walsall, came noisily down the street. Their purpose was to capture Wesley. The Darlaston crowd were angry and now tried to protect him, but they were no match for the ferocity and toughness of the Walsall gang. There was a fight and several Darlaston men were knocked down and hurt. The rest ran away. He was left standing alone on the chair, and for once it was no use his saying anything. His voice was drowned in the roar of the fight and the fierce shouts of the men from Walsall.

Strong hands reached up and dragged him from the chair. Two men gripped him hard and pulled him roughly down the street towards Walsall. Rain was pouring down, and John, who always loved being smartly dressed, was now drenched, muddy and very bedraggled. He made one despairing effort to escape, and almost wriggled free and into the door of a house. But a man grabbed him by his hair (it was a pity John did not follow the fashion of those days and wear a wig. He might have escaped then!). He was pulled roughly back into the crowd.

As usual he tried to speak, but the crowd shouted, 'Knock his brains out!' 'Down with him!' 'Kill him at once!' Things looked grim, but suddenly he managed to say a few words, and these words won him his first friend in the gang. He was an important friend because he was the local prize fighter and butcher! He was so impressed with the little man's courage and with his words, that he changed sides in two minutes.

'No one shall touch a hair of your head,' he roared.

The surprised thugs drew back. The little preacher was one thing. The gigantic prize-fighter was very different. John's new supporter took him safely back to the house in Darlaston, where John found he had a scratch on the hand, a torn waistcoat, very wet clothes and nothing worse.

John's courage as well as his words made the boxer and many others think about Jesus for the first time in their lives. If you could have seen him I don't think you would have ever guessed this small, neatly dressed man with well-combed hair, who had been a professor at Oxford University, could possibly have spent most of his life outside in sunshine, in snow, in rain, in gales, speaking to men and women who had never seen the inside of a church, about Jesus and about the need to turn from their sins to a Saviour. If he had just had the bravery of a prize fighter he couldn't have done it, but he was brave because he knew that his job had been given to him by God, and that therefore God would give him all the strength and courage he needed.

For fifty-three years he travelled the muddy, bumpy roads of Britain till he died at the age of eighty-eight in 1791. He left little money, but he left thousands who mourned him, and many followers, who are called Methodists.

In his lifetime there had been great Prime Ministers and great generals, but no one had changed England so much as the brave John Wesley, the boy rescued from the flames.

From London, with Love

Gladys Aylward was born in London in 1902. She lived with her parents, and when she was old enough they took her to church and sent her to Sunday School. She left school when she was fourteen years old and, after several other jobs, she became a parlourmaid in a house in the West End of London.

Gladys had one big ambition in life and that was to be an actress. Quite often in the evenings, when she had finished her work, she would go to drama classes.

One evening Gladys was invited to attend a service at a local church. She agreed to go, and during the sermon she heard the preacher say that the time would come when everyone would have to stand before God and give an account of the way they'd lived their lives. During the next few days Gladys thought about what she had heard at the church and she decided to accept Jesus Christ as her Saviour, and let him take charge of her life.

Soon after this, she read an article about China which said that there were millions of Chinese people who had never heard of Jesus Christ. Gladys was amazed. Someone should do something about this. She thought about what she had read, and decided that God wanted her to go to China as a missionary. This seemed to be far more important than being an actress.

Gladys was not sure how to become a missionary, and she was told to apply to the China Inland Mission. The society accepted her application and sent Gladys on a three-month training course. Everything seemed to be going well, but when the course was over Gladys was shocked to find out that she wasn't to be invited back for further training. The society explained that they thought Gladys would be unable to learn Chinese, which was one of the most difficult languages in the world.

This was a terrible blow for Gladys. What was she to do? In the months which followed she tried to find out what God's plans for her were. She was still determined to go to China. At last she had an idea. She would save up all her money and buy herself a ticket to China. She did extra work to earn more money, and she saved every penny she earned. Gladys also found out that the cheapest and quickest way to China was to go by train through Europe, Russia and Siberia to a place called Tientsin. At last she had enough money and she went along to the travel agent and bought her ticket. It cost £47 10s. Now she could start her journey to China.

* * * *

It was October 15th, 1932 and Gladys woke up feeling excited and rather frightened. She was excited because today she was to start her journey to China. She was going to leave her home, her family, and her friends and go to the other side of the world. That was what made her feel frightened! China was a long way away and the train journey would take about three weeks. Gladys wasn't used to travelling. The furthest away from home she had ever been before was on a day trip to the Isle of Wight. Gladys tried to picture the maps she'd looked at, and remember the names of all the countries she would go through. Would she ever reach China safely? Would everything be all right when she arrived at the border of Manchuria, where there was a war taking place? What about all those foreign languages? Gladys could only speak English. It was too late to change her mind now. Today she was starting her journey to China.

Gladys arrived at Liverpool Street Station, London, carrying two suitcases. One case was filled with food, and the other contained clothes, a sleeping bag, a kettle, a saucepan, and a small spirit stove. Gladys had no extra money to buy food on the journey, so she had to take all her supplies with her. She said goodbye to the few friends and relations who had come to the station with her, and climbed into the train. Minutes later, the train steamed slowly out of the station and Gladys was on her way.

When they reached Harwich, Gladys got on a boat that was going to Flushing, in Holland. As the boat set sail, Gladys watched the coast of England fade into the distance, and suddenly she felt very lonely. She soon cheered herself up. God wanted her in China, and that's where she was going.

In Holland Gladys got on another train, and started the next stage of her journey to Tientsin.

When she had been on Liverpool Street Station, Gladys had noticed a man and a woman boarding the train. The man had a small beard. These two people were already in the carriage when Gladys got on the train at Flushing, and she sat down opposite them. The lady smiled and said, 'Didn't we see you at Liverpool Street?'

'Yes,' replied Gladys, surprised to hear an English voice.

'Where are you going?' asked the lady.

'I'm going to China.'

The couple were most surprised to hear this.

'What on earth are you going there for?'

'I want to tell the Chinese about Jesus Christ.'

Both of them stared at Gladys, and at that moment an attendant appeared at the door. The lady spoke in French and the attendant went away. A few minutes later, he came back carrying three cups of chocolate and a plate of biscuits.

'Do join us,' said the lady. Gladys was happy to do so. The three of them talked quietly together until the couple got off the train, and Gladys was left on her own.

When the train crossed the border into Germany, a railway official tried to ask Gladys some questions. No matter how hard she tried, Gladys couldn't understand a word he said. Eventually a German girl, who spoke some English, came to the rescue and explained that the man wanted to know if she had anything to declare at the customs. The German girl was very kind to Gladys, and when they reached Berlin she invited Gladys to her house for the night.

The next morning the girl showed Gladys round the city, before she set off on the next stage of her journey via Warsaw and Moscow to Harbin.

The journey to Warsaw was uneventful. As the train left Warsaw and sped towards Russia, Gladys noticed that soldiers seemed to be everywhere, and they even searched the train. As the journey continued, water became more difficult to obtain. At the stations Gladys would run along the platform to join the other passengers filling up their pots and buckets from a tap.

She arrived at Moscow and had to change trains. Again there were lots of soldiers around the station, and Gladys thought the people looked dirty and unhappy. Once on the train heading for China, Gladys cheered up. She had to share a compartment with three men, but they were all very polite. The train steamed on across the silent countryside.

One day Gladys woke up feeling very lonely. She opened up her Bible and read one of the Psalms and this made her feel a bit better. To keep her spirits up she sang hymns, and the other people in the carriage seemed to enjoy this, even though they couldn't understand what Gladys was singing about.

One day a man got into the compartment who could speak some English. Gladys was very pleased to be able to talk to someone. The carriage fairly buzzed with conversation, for the other passengers wanted to know all about Gladys, and the man had to act as an interpreter. Before the man got off the train, he gave Gladys a message from the guard. There were no trains running to Harbin, the junction where Gladys had to change on to the Manchurian railway, because another train had been captured by the Japanese and the line was blocked.

In spite of several warnings, which she didn't understand, Gladys stayed on the train, even when all the other passengers, apart from the soldiers, got off. The train went on all day and in the evening it stopped again. The soldiers got out and Gladys was alone.

Suddenly there was the sound of gunfire, and Gladys realized that she had reached the fighting line and the train would go no further. She gathered up all her belongings and stepped out on to the deserted platform. Gladys was cold, miserable and hungry. She thought of her home back in England and wondered if she would ever reach Tientsin. At one end of the platform there was a small hut. Inside the hut were four men – the guard, the engine driver, the fireman and the station porter. Apparently the train was to stay at the station for the moment. Then it would be used to carry the wounded back to the nearest big town. The men didn't know how long they would have to wait. They gave Gladys some coffee, and then she picked up her things and started off on the long walk back down the line.

What a walk! It was dark, it was snowing and there were wolves howling in the nearby woods. At about midnight, Gladys stopped to make some coffee and have something to eat. Then she lay down on her suitcases, wrapped her fur coat around her, and tried to get some sleep. She walked all the next day, and reached the town in the evening. She put her bags on the platform and sat down.

Soon some soldiers came up to Gladys and, taking her luggage, they marched her off to be searched. Gladys was terrified. She took out her Bible and as she did so a small piece of paper fell out of it. The paper was from an old calendar and on it were the words 'Be ye not afraid of them – I am your God', a verse from the Old Testament. This cheered Gladys up, and she remembered that it was God's wish she should go to China. If God wanted her in China, then God would make sure she arrived safely!

At first the soldiers tried to persuade Gladys to stay in the town, but when they realized that she was determined to go on, they put her on another train with instructions about where to change for Harbin. When Gladys got off this train she was told that the Japanese had closed in, and all the lines to Harbin were blocked. What was she to do now? As Gladys sat on the station, she saw a sight she would never forget. About fifty people – men, women and girls – were chained together by their hands and feet, and were being driven along by the soldiers. Many of them were in tears. They were being taken to Siberia to work in the labour camps.

Gladys spent the night on the station and next morning a train arrived heading back the way she had come. Gladys saw a man looking out of one of the windows. In desperation she cried, 'Can you tell me how to get to Harbin?' To her surprise the man replied in English, 'You can't, it's blocked. Go to Vladivostok.'

Gladys got a train to Vladivostok without much

difficulty. Once in the city though, she found it hard to leave. The Russians would not let her go to China, and they tried to persuade her to stay in Russia. Eventually, Gladys got help and was put on board a ship going to Japan. When the boat reached Japan, Gladys was one of the first to go ashore and she was handed over to the British Consulate.

Although Gladys was very fond of Japan, she was anxious to continue her journey. On November 5th, she sailed for China, and arrived at Tientsin on November 10th. At once she made her way to the local missionary headquarters. Gladys was given a warm welcome and the mission held a special service of thanksgiving. One of the hymns they sang was 'Praise, my soul, the King of heaven'. Gladys meant every word. She had arrived in China.

Gladys did succeed in learning the Chinese language and the courage she showed throughout her life made her one of the best known missionaries of the twentieth century.

Flight to Death

The little yellow plane circled slowly above the dense tropical jungle. The dark green tree tops stretched as far as the eye could see in every direction, broken occasionally by chocolate-coloured rivers snaking through the trees. Underneath the umbrella-like tree tops, lived the Auca tribe, hidden by the forest which was their home.

'Fuel's getting low,' stated Nate, the pilot. 'I'll make one more turn; if we can't see anything then, we'll have to return to Arajuno.'

He ran his eyes carefully over the seemingly unbroken sea of trees. Were the Aucas there? Were they searching in the right place?

'Look,' exclaimed Jim Elliot, his passenger, 'over there – a clearing – several of them.'

He was right. The break in the tree tops was a good-sized clearing, surrounded by several others.

'It's them!' he exclaimed, 'We've found them.'

'I'm keeping my height,' said the pilot, 'in case we frighten them.'

They circled over the village a few more times, and then set their course west back to Arajuno, their thoughts full of the Aucas and their discovery.

* * * *

The Aucas are a small tribe, about 1,000 in number, living in a large area of dense jungle. The name Auca means 'savage' and at this time they certainly lived up to their name.

Don Carlos sold rubber, which he found in the jungle in Auca country. He had had several narrow escapes from the Aucas since his arrival in Ecuador and he had learnt quite a lot about their methods.

'They attack by surprise,' he told Nate and Jim, 'and always in large groups. They wait at the bend of a river and when the current pushes your boat close to the shore, they hurl spears and shout blood-curdling yells to confuse you. It happened to me once just like that. Dozens of them there were. The canoe capsized and five Indians with me were killed immediately. I managed to kill two Aucas and escaped through a hail of spears. It took me eight days to get home – and I was lucky to recover.

'I remember once finding a deserted Auca hut. In it was a lifesized human figure carved of balsa wood. But that's not all. The head and face were marked out in red, and the whole figure was torn with spear marks. Nine-foot spears they use – with deadly skill.'

Nate and Jim looked at each other. This was what they had come to Ecuador for; to find the Aucas and tell them about Jesus Christ. It was a terrifying prospect. No group of men had ever entered Auca country and come out unharmed. What was driving Nate and Jim to do this?

When Nate was seven, his older brother took him flying. He was so small that he had to stand on the seat to see out of the cockpit! From that time on, his one ambition was to be a pilot, and he thought of little else. It seemed the end of the world to Nate when he failed to pass the Air Force medical. What was he to do if he couldn't fly? He asked God what he should do, and after much training and practice, Nate arrived in Ecuador convinced that God wanted him to run a 'Flying Doctor' service in the jungle.

Jim had not met Nate until he arrived in Ecuador. Like Nate, he had been a Christian since he was at school, where he was successful at work and sport – especially wrestling. Many people were surprised when Jim announced that he was not going to follow his planned career, but was going to Ecuador as a missionary.

Was it right for these men to risk their lives for a few savages? Nate asked himself this question as he sat at his typewriter one evening at Shell Mera, his base in Ecuador. Unless they told the Aucas about the Lord Jesus Christ, the savages would die without ever having heard God's message of love and forgiveness. The two men believed God had commanded them to tell the Aucas, and they had to obey.

* * * *

Nate and Jim had found out where the Aucas lived. Now they had to make contact. Their plan was to drop gifts from the aeroplane to the Aucas and shout messages to the tribespeople, such as, 'I want to be your friend.'

They had an ingenious way of dropping gifts. A

fifteen-hundred-foot line was lowered from a circling aeroplane. A bucket on the end of this line remained still below the 'plane, and gifts could be taken out or put in.

They did this several times over the Auca village, sending down brightly coloured buttons, kettles, knives and clothes. Gradually, the Aucas became less nervous. Their curiosity made them run out to see the aeroplane and collect their gifts. Later, they began to wave and give gifts themselves – head-bands of feathers, a parrot and a chicken. They seemed almost friendly.

Other people before had tried to win the friend-ship of the tribe, and from their stories Nate and Jim knew that they had to move very carefully. Their next step was to find a landing place in Auca country. A sand-bank on the river seemed the most likely place, and after some searching, a suitable one was found a little way from the Auca village. They called it Palm Beach. Landing would be tricky and take-off even worse, but Nate thought it was possible.

Three of their friends offered to join Nate and Jim to help with 'Operation Auca'. Plans were finalized and a date fixed for the move in to Palm Beach – January 3rd, 1956.

They were excited. This was why they had come to Ecuador. Nobody before had told the Aucas about Jesus Christ. Now was their opportunity. What was going to happen? Would the Aucas be as savage as ever? Or were they going to be friendly?

The morning of Tuesday, January 3rd, dawned

bright. Nate had not slept much that night. He was worried about the plane and the landing. If anything went wrong, he would be stranded right in the middle of a jungle, surrounded by Aucas. He pushed these worries to the back of his mind, determined to go ahead with things now.

He checked the plane, and then went inside for breakfast and a final prayer before starting.

Nate took off with Ed, one of the three men who had joined them, at eight o'clock. It was misty, but it cleared as they approached their landing site, and after a practice run, Nate landed safely on Palm Beach. A landing was possible. The two men jumped out, happy that the first obstacle was past. Now there was the take-off to worry about. The sand was soft, but Nate made it, waved to Ed, who had stayed below, and set off back.

On the next flight, Nate flew in Jim and Roger (another friend), a radio set and some food. All went well, and he returned for flight number three – boards for a tree-house and table. The men built a rough shelter for the night, while Nate made two more flights with food and materials.

As he took off to return home in the evening, he flew low over the Auca village, and called out over a loudspeaker, 'Come to the river to-morrow.'

The night was hot. Pumas roamed the beach below the men who slept in their tree-house under mosquito nets. When Nate arrived on Wednesday morning, he found Jim and his two friends walking up and down the beach, shouting welcoming messages to the Aucas. All was quiet, however, for the rest of that day.

Another night and day passed. The men waited for the Aucas to come, but there was no sign of them. All was still, so still, in fact, that they felt sure they were being watched. Then Nate, flying low over the river, saw some footprints in the sand a little way below the camp. This livened things up a bit. The Aucas were coming nearer. Again, they flew over the Auca village.

'Come to the river,' they shouted.

And on Friday they came – three of them – one man and two women. They were curious and unafraid. One of them even went for a trip in Nate's plane, flying low over his village and waving, to the astonishment of his friends.

The next day was disappointing. No one came. They had been at Palm Beach now for five days and they had met three Aucas. Nate, back at Arajuno that night, felt that the next day would be *the* day. He flew low over the Auca village in the morning, and to his surprise, found only a few people there. The rest were on their way to Palm Beach, he told the others as he landed. He radioed Marj, his wife, with the news.

'Pray for us,' he finished, 'This *is* the day. We'll contact you next at four-thirty.'

* * * *

At four-thirty, Marj Saint switched on her radio set. She was excited. What was the news?

She waited. Four-thirty passed and no message

came. The other wives were listening.

'No message yet?' they asked.

'No word yet. We're standing by,' replied Marj.

There was still no word by sunset, and they slept little that night.

The women had their first news at nine-thirty the next morning. Another missionary pilot flew low over Palm Beach. He saw no sign of the men – only a wrecked plane on the beach.

A search party was organized. The United States Air Force sent in 'planes and a team. Later that week, the bodies of the men were found brutally murdered by the Aucas.

A funeral service was held at Palm Beach in a tropical thunderstorm, and the search party returned.

They reported that the footprints on the beach showed that there had been a struggle. The plane was wrecked, the covering ripped off, the framework bent and seats torn up.

Nate and Jim and their three friends had known just what the Aucas were like, and so had their wives. Yet, in spite of these fears, they were sure God had told them to go to the Aucas with the good news of Jesus Christ. They chose to obey God, and showed great courage. Nate saw it like this. If a man enters the army, he must be willing to give up everything, even his life, for his country. It is the same with the Lord Jesus. When he asks us to join his army, we must be prepared to give up everything, even life itself, for him.

Nurse Among the Rebels

All around was jungle. Great, tall trees cut out the light of the sun, long creepers trailed from them to the ground, and huge curtains of green leaves hung above. Deep nestling in the jungle was a camp. Some Africans were cooking over a fire. Others were getting ready for the night. Sitting in the middle, and looking a little out of place, was an English lady. She was slimly built, had fair hair and was wearing glasses. Her dress was muddy and torn in places and her legs were badly bruised and grazed. Her name was Margaret Hayes.

'The supper is ready,' a slim young African girl whispered. 'Come and eat after your journey.' She handed Margaret a bowl of food in which was boiled rice and Margaret ate it hungrily.

There was hardly any noise in the camp. Everyone kept as silent as possible and talked in whispers. They could never be sure how near the rebel army was. If the rebels found them, they would almost certainly shoot them, especially as there was a white woman with them, and the rebels said that all whites were their enemies. Margaret felt very frightened, but tried not to show it.

She had just finished her meal when a man dashed into the camp. His face was glossy with sweat and he had a look of fear in his eyes. 'The enemy are getting closer,' he said. 'We shall have to move the white lady.' Everyone was afraid and chattered nervously.

One of Margaret's friends, Bo, arrived next morning; 'Come with me,' he said with a face that looked worried and grey. Margaret bustled round to collect her things. Soon they were creeping off through the forest, wading through mud and pools of water and and ducking under the swaying creepers. After a short distance, they met another friend named Paul. 'Margaret,' he said with a look of misery on his face, 'there is something I must tell you.'

Margaret's heart began to beat faster as she tried to think what it might be. 'Tell me. What is it?'

'We have just heard that your friends are dead. I'm sorry, Margaret. The rebels have shot them all.'

'All of them?' She could not really take it in. All of her friends, including Mary Baker, the person she had been working with all these years in the Congo, all dead.

'Yes, Margaret, all of them, and they are after your life as well. That is why we must take you and hide you somewhere safer.'

They plunged on through the tangled jungle undergrowth. Before long, Bo Martin led her to a small hide-out they were preparing. When they arrived, all Margaret could do was flop into the chair they had brought from the village. She felt exhausted and very unhappy. The only thing that comforted her was the fact that she knew her friends would be in heaven now with Jesus. The puzzle was why God had not let her be killed too. She put her head in her hands and prayed, 'Dear God, please help me to carry on and serve you whatever happens,

and even though I do not understand it.'

Days passed in the jungle hide-out. Sometimes the rebel soldiers came quite close. They had to keep absolutely silent while they searched nearby and then, when they had moved away a little, Margaret and Bo Martin moved to another hiding place. One day after a lot of scrambling through the jungle to get away from the rebels, a messenger came panting up to them. He gasped, getting his breath back. 'They've killed two of the villagers,' he said. 'They say they'll kill more until we hand the white woman over to them. Also they've burnt the houses of the village.' This was terrible news for Margaret. The last thing she wanted was to harm her friends. The messenger went on, 'They are very angry that we have not given up the white woman.'

That night Margaret could not get to sleep. She thought and thought about the villagers who had died and suffered because of her. She asked God to give her courage to trust him and do what was right. When morning came at last and the sun began to show through the trees, she knew what she was going to do.

'Bo,' she said, 'I am going to give myself up to the rebels. Will you come and lead me to their base?' Bo Martin tried to persuade her not to go, but she was certain she was right.

Two hours later, a very bedraggled English lady, her face dirty, her hair a tangled mess and her clothes torn and filthy, walked slowly into the village where the rebel base was. As she stumbled into an open space surrounded by huts, she heard excited chattering sounds and soon a mass of people surrounded her, some asking questions, some shouting insults. Margaret stood there quietly. She felt very tired. After a while, a kind man brought a chair which she thankfully sank on to. She knew it would not be long before the rebels discovered she was there and then, she thought, they would not waste much time before they killed her.

Soon above the noise of talking, she began to make out the steady rumble of a lorry. The sound got louder and then the lorry swept into the clearing. Some rebel soldiers, all wearing red arm bands but no other proper uniform, leapt out of the lorry, immediately came towards Margaret and hustled her into the back of the lorry. They roared off and took her to the house where the major was living. They pushed her inside and then left her standing in the middle of a group of soldiers, while those who had brought her went to report to the major.

The major was not free to see her straightaway. While they were waiting, some of the young rebels danced round her, calling her names and trying to make her afraid. One came up to her and said, grinning, 'I've been told that I'm the one who will cut your throat!' He brandished a long sharp gleaming hunting knife. 'You're a Protestant missionary, aren't you? Well then, you won't mind dying as you believe you will go to heaven.'

'That's right,' said Margaret quietly. 'I hope you believe that too.'

'Are you afraid to die?'

'No.' She was not afraid. She had prayed a lot

about this, and God was giving her the courage to face death.

The soldier gazed at her thoughtfully for a moment. 'You know, I really think I believe you.'

After an hour of waiting the major appeared. He was a short, plump man of about fifty with a kind-looking face. He was wearing khaki shorts, a sleeveless jacket, a leopard skin and a string of lucky charms, including a human thumb! He shouted a sharp command and a chair was brought for the exhausted missionary to sit on.

'Are you the white woman we have been trying to capture all this time? Where have you been? How did you get here?'

'I am the white woman you've been searching for. I have given myself up because I don't want any more of the village people to be killed because of me. If you want to kill me, go ahead, but don't kill my friends.' It will soon be over, thought Margaret. Now they will kill me.

There was a long silence, but the order to shoot did not come. Instead the major said, 'You are not going to die. We want you to work.' And so, once again, for some reason she could not understand, Margaret found that God had saved her life.

Some months later, a large but battered American car roared into the little town of Buta and pulled up outside the women's convent there. Several people got out of the car, among them Margaret. Soon the nuns came out, welcomed her and took her inside. The convent was light and airy and clean. Margaret immediately began to feel better. She had spent so long in filthy, disgusting places with the rebels that it was a great relief to sit down to a delightful peaceful meal off a clean plate, and then afterwards go up to a little bedroom which she had all to herself, have a thorough wash and snuggle down between beautiful clean white sheets.

But the time of peace and quiet did not last long. She and the nuns, too, were still prisoners of the rebels and one morning the soldiers came to destroy the peace of the convent. They stormed through the building, shouting and yelling. They quickly rounded up the frightened nuns and Margaret, prodding them with rifles. The soldiers pushed the women outside and up the dusty road to a men's convent a short distance away. Outside the convent they saw that the rebels had made the priests sit cross-legged in rows. Some of the priests were strong young men; others were old and wrinkled with white hair. Rebel guards strode up and down the rows. Now that the women had arrived, they shouted at the priests to get up. Then they ordered both women and men to march down the road again.

After marching for about ten minutes they reached a drab tumbledown building which had once been a police station. When everyone was assembled, the rebels searched them carefully taking away anything that looked at all valuable. They took away Margaret's glasses, so that from then on all she could see was blurred shapes. The leader of the soldiers shouted, 'Halt! Now get inside.' They moved in slowly one by one through a door which creaked on its hinges as they pushed it open. Inside, dirty yellow paint was peeling off the walls, and strips of it hung down from the ceiling. Many of the windows were broken and cracked. Two benches and two old tables were the only things in the room. As they searched, they laughed at the prisoners and tried to make them look ridiculous. Margaret tried to comfort herself by remembering what Jesus went through on the cross. She prayed that he would save them, but even more that he would give her the courage to bear anything they did to her.

At long last the search was finished and the prisoners were allowed to lie down on the floor and try to sleep. The door was locked and guards stood outside. The night dawdled past. Few could sleep properly. They all spent some of the time praying. Everyone, of course, was wondering what was going to happen to them. As the light of dawn flooded into the dreary room, the door opened and a rebel guard entered.

'Men, get outside. Women, stand round the walls,' he commanded. Silently, the priests filed out of the door, while the nuns and Margaret moved to the walls. They could hear the priests being led away. A few moments later the door flew open and an officer burst into the room. 'The Colonel has sentenced the priests to death,' he said. 'But don't you worry. The Colonel says he won't kill you yet. Just relax and don't be afraid.' Later that day, straining their ears the women could hear shouts in the distance and the stutter of a machine gun. Then they knew that every one of the priests was dead.

It would have been terribly easy for Margaret to panic and despair, to think that God was no longer looking after her. But she did not give up or lose heart. She went on praying for strength and that she and the others would be set free. As it turned out, they had to wait quite a few more weeks but eventually the day did come when rescuers came, fought off the rebels and took Margaret and the nuns to safety. And as she looked back on the terrible times she had been through, she could see how God had answered her prayers – he had given her the courage to face the troubles and he had set her free. She thanked God for that.